A TREE IS NICE

by

JANICE MAY UDRY

pictures by

MARC SIMONT

HarperCollins*Publishers*

Trees are very nice. They fill up the sky.

They go beside the rivers and down the
valleys. They live up on the hills.

Trees make the woods.
They make everything beautiful.

Even if you have just one tree, it is nice too.
A tree is nice because it has leaves. The leaves
whisper in the breeze all summer long.

In the fall, the leaves come down and we play in them. We walk in the leaves and roll in the leaves.

We build playhouses out of the leaves. Then we pile them up with our rakes and have a bonfire.

A tree is nice because it has a trunk and limbs.
We can climb the tree and see over all the yards.
We can sit on a limb and think about things.
Or play pirate ship up in the tree.

If it is an apple tree we can climb it
to pick the apples.

Cats get away from dogs by going up the tree.
Birds build nests in trees and live there.
Sticks come off the trees too.
We draw in the sand with the sticks.

A tree is nice to hang a swing in.

Or a basket of flowers.

It is a good place to lean your hoe while you rest.

A tree is nice because it makes shade.

The cows lie down in the shade when it is hot.

People have picnics there too. And the baby takes his nap in his buggy in the shade.

A tree is nice for a house to be near.
The tree shades the house and keeps it cool.

The tree holds off the wind and keeps the wind
from blowing the roof off the house sometimes.

A tree is nice to plant. You dig the biggest
hole you can and put the little tree in.
Then you pour in lots of water and then the dirt.
You hang the shovel back in the garage.

Every day for years and YEARS
you watch the little tree grow.
You say to people, "I planted that tree."

They wish they had one so they
go home and plant a tree too.